ESPORTS: GREATEST MOMENTS

ESPORTS LIVE

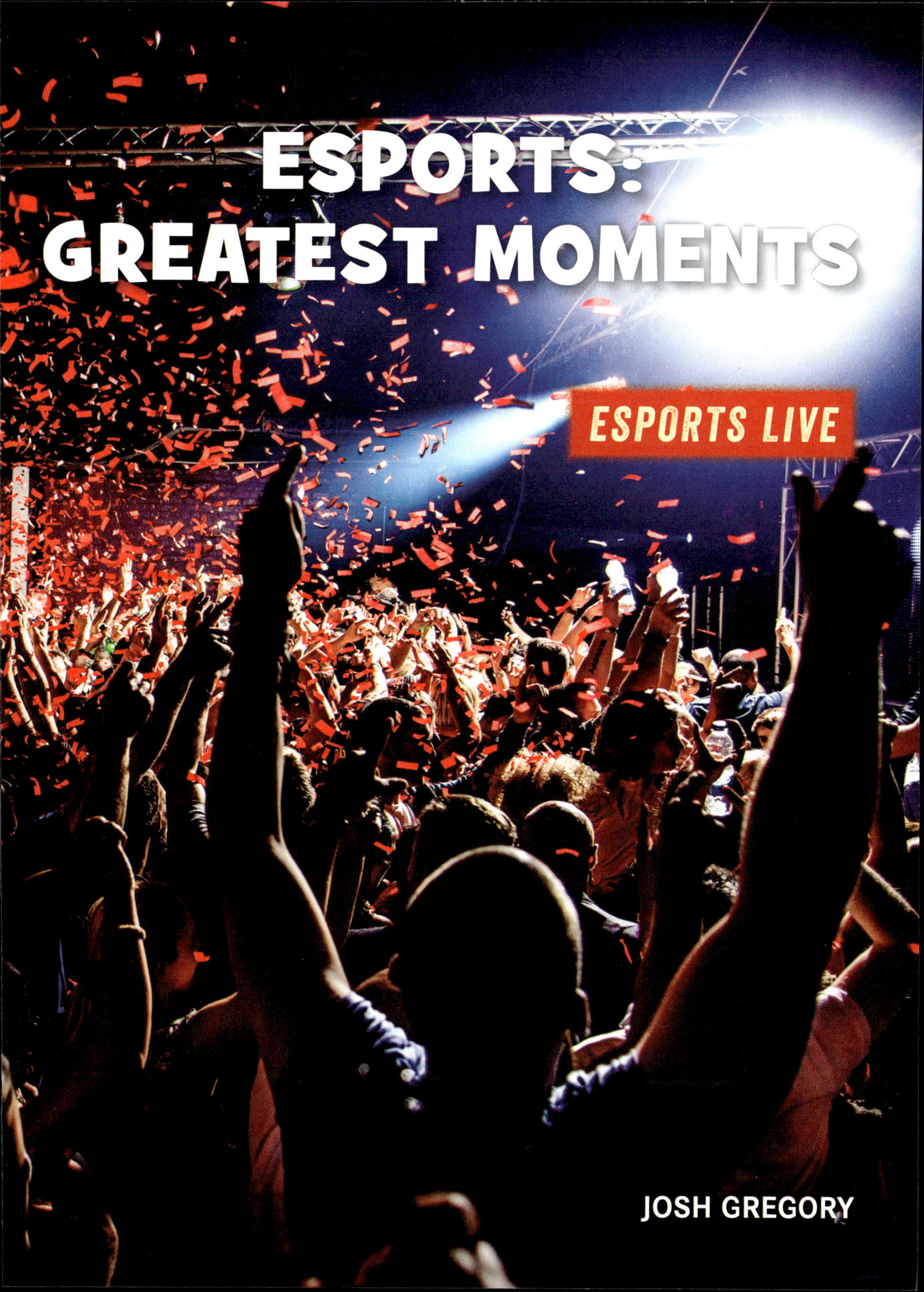

JOSH GREGORY

CHERRY LAKE PRESS

Published in the United States of America by Cherry Lake Publishing Group
Ann Arbor, Michigan
www.cherrylakepublishing.com

Reading Adviser: Marla Conn, MS, Ed., Literacy specialist, Read-Ability, Inc.
Photo Credits: © Anthony Mooney/Shutterstock.com, cover, 1; © ESL [Stephanie Lieske], 5;
   © ESL [Helena Kristiansson], 6; © ESL [Adela Sznajder], 9, 11, 26; © ESL [Bart Oerbekke], 12, 13;
   © Leonel Calara/Shutterstock.com, 14; © Dmitriy Kuzietsov/Shutterstock.com, 17; © ESL [Carlton
   Beener], 19; © dpa picture alliance/Alamy Stock Photo, 20, 21; © Gorodenkoff/Shutterstock.com, 22;
   © Kobby Dagan/Shutterstock.com, 25; © ESL [Viola Schuldner], 28

Cherry Lake Press is an imprint of Cherry Lake Publishing Group.

Library of Congress Cataloging-in-Publication Data
Names: Gregory, Josh, author.
Title: Esports. Greatest moments / Josh Gregory.
Description: Ann Arbor, Michigan : Cherry Lake Publishing, 2021 | Series: Esports live | Includes index. |
   Audience: Grades 4-6
Identifiers: LCCN 2020002738 (print) | LCCN 2020002739 (ebook) | ISBN 9781534168862 (hardcover) |
   ISBN 9781534170544 (paperback) | ISBN 9781534172388 (pdf) | ISBN 9781534174221 (ebook)
Subjects: LCSH: eSports (Contests)—History—Juvenile literature.
Classification: LCC GV1469.34.E86 G74 2021 (print) | LCC GV1469.34.E86 (ebook) | DDC 794.8—dc23
LC record available at https://lccn.loc.gov/2020002738
LC ebook record available at https://lccn.loc.gov/2020002739

Cherry Lake Publishing Group would like to acknowledge the work of the Partnership for 21st Century
Learning, a Network of Battelle for Kids. Please visit http://www.battelleforkids.org/networks/p21
for more information.

Printed in the United States of America
Corporate Graphics

ABOUT THE AUTHOR

Josh Gregory is the author of more than 150 books for kids. He has written about everything
from animals to technology to history. A graduate of the University of Missouri–Columbia,
he currently lives in Chicago, Illinois.

TABLE OF CONTENTS

CHAPTER 1

When the Crowd Goes Wild

The most dramatic moments in sports can make history. If you watch **esports**, you know that professional video game competitions can be just as thrilling as traditional sports. And even though esports are still new, they have already seen their fair share of legendary moments.

Sports are a natural source of drama. Sometimes it comes from the specific events of a match. Other times, a moment is exciting because it's simply never happened before. A big part of the fun also comes from following the personal stories of your favorite players and teams. Esports competitors go through

Even the players get excited during esports tournaments.

a lot to make it big. They spend countless hours training and make sacrifices to become great at their chosen games. And sometimes they have to overcome big obstacles in their lives as they make their way to the top. It is inspiring to watch these people succeed, and their personal stories give fans an extra reason to root for them.

The lights and music help add to the drama of an esports event.

The most memorable moments of all come from some combination of these exciting situations. When an underdog player comes from behind to win a championship match. When a team pulls off an incredible play to win a record-setting prize. When a young player becomes the first person from their home country to win a major event. These are the things people won't just be talking about for the next day or the next week. These moments will live on for as long as people discuss esports.

Looking Back

Have you ever heard about an incredible match that happened before you started following esports? Just because you weren't able to see it live doesn't mean you can't enjoy it anyway. Many of esports' greatest hits are available to watch over and over again on YouTube and other video sites. It can be a lot of fun to look up matches from decades past. It's also a great way to see how far esports have come since then!

CHAPTER 2

Coming from Behind

Fighting game tournaments were among the first esports events to find a wider audience. Over the past 20 years, these tournaments have grown bigger and bigger. It makes a lot of sense that fighting games are so popular in the world of esports. Most of them require players to face each other one-on-one. This can lead to intense **rivalries** and drama around each match, much like boxing or other head-to-head competitions. Fighting game matches also tend to be very short, and it is easy to see who is winning. The goal in almost every fighting game is simply to bring the opponent's health meter down to zero. Even beginners can understand the basics, so anyone can have fun watching a good match.

It's up to the **commentators** to narrate the event to viewers in the audience and at home.

Perhaps the most famous match in fighting game history took place at the 2004 Evolution Championship Series, better known to fans as simply Evo. Evo is one of the world's biggest fighting game tournaments. Each year, players come from all over the world to show their skills at a variety of different fighting games.

At the 2004 tournament, two of the world's most well-known *Street Fighter* players faced off for the first time during the semifinals for *Street Fighter III: 3rd Strike*. Daigo Umehara from

Street Fighter originally released in the 1990s.

Teams play for huge cash prizes and trophies.

Tokyo, Japan, was set to battle Justin Wong of New York City. Each had already found fame and fans in the fighting game community, and spectators couldn't wait to see what happened when they met for the first time.

Wong chose to play as the character Chun-Li, while Umehara selected Ken. To win the match, one of them would have to win two out of three possible rounds. They split the first two rounds between them, which meant everything was on the line for round three. Wong had a strong start. He played defensively, bringing

Some pro gamers can make up to 10 moves in 1 second.

Umehara's health bar all the way down to a tiny sliver while keeping his own character in fairly good shape.

That's when the action really got started. Wong launched one of Chun-Li's most powerful moves, which was made up of 15 very fast kicks in a row. If any one of these hits made contact with Umehara's character, the match would've been over.

Umehara reacted with lightning-fast reflexes. Instead of trying to avoid the attack, he decided to **parry**. This meant he would have to press a button with split-second accuracy each time one

At tournaments, actors and fans will dress up like players in the game.

Daigo Umehara has won several Guinness World Records
for his gaming accomplishments.

of the kicks was about to hit his character. The amount of time he had to press the button each time was less than one-tenth of a second. The crowd at the tournament went wild as Umehara pulled off this incredible feat 15 times in a row, avoiding all potential damage. He then immediately launched his own **combo**, wiping out Wong's entire remaining health bar in seconds and winning the match. It was a remarkable come-from-behind victory that required immense skills to pull off.

Umehara ended up losing the tournament in the finals, but it didn't matter. The "Daigo Parry" immediately went down in history as one of the greatest fighting game accomplishments ever. YouTube videos of the match continue to get millions of views even today.

Words of Wisdom

Daigo Umehara is a well-known celebrity in his home country of Japan. He even wrote a best-selling book called The Will to Keep Winning. *In it, he provides general life advice and reveals the secrets to his success. Many up-and-coming fighting game players turn to the book for inspiration as they try to become as successful as Umehara.*

CHAPTER 3

A Lot on the Line

Multiplayer online battle arenas, or MOBAs, have also been popular as esports for some time. One of the biggest is *Dota 2*. Its annual championship tournament, the International, draws huge numbers of viewers and offers record-setting cash prizes. Millions of dollars can be on the line during an International finals match.

At the 2015 International, the American team Evil Geniuses faced off against China's CDEC in the finals. In this three-out-of-five series, Evil Geniuses were up two matches to one. But at the start of the fourth match, it looked like CDEC might even the odds. CDEC defeated one of the five Evil Genius players and

Evil Geniuses was founded in 1999, and has teams for various games including *Dota 2*, *League of Legends*, and more.

then set out to attack a computer-controlled monster. By defeating the monster, they would gain a variety of useful bonuses. But the remaining four Evil Genius players had other plans.

The five CDEC players were packed tightly together in a small area as they fought the monster. The Evil Geniuses soon showed up to surprise them, and they had a perfect plan. They set off a series of special abilities that worked together very well. For example, one player used an ability that slowed down the CDEC players and increased the amount of damage they took from magic attacks. The next player launched a magic attack to take advantage of this. Finally, one of the players used a move called the Echo Slam. It stuns enemies and does extra damage when multiple players are near each other. Because all of the CDEC players were trapped in a tight space, the attack hit all of them, creating huge damage. It also stunned them in place long enough for follow-up attacks to take out four of their five players.

Only one CDEC player escaped. In the meantime, the Evil Geniuses took out the computer-controlled monster, winning all the bonuses. They won the round soon after, securing the International championship and walking away with more than $6 million. *Dota 2* fans still consider it one of the most exciting events in the game's history.

Crowds are excited to meet their favorite players.

Close to 200 players made it to the 2019 *Fortnite* World Cup finals in New York.

The minimum age to compete in the *Fortnite* World Cup was 13.

In 2019, Epic Games held the first-ever *Fortnite* World Cup. Because *Fortnite* is so popular, more people were paying attention to the tournament than perhaps any previous esports event. Thousands of people participated, and millions more followed the action on streaming sites. For the players who made it to the finals in New York City, the pressure was incredible. The winner would

Too much screen time can be harmful. Blue light from computers and TVs can cause headaches and blurry vision.

take home more than $3 million and go down in history as the first-ever *Fortnite* World Cup champion. And with so many people watching, every move they made was sure to be picked apart and analyzed. Mistakes and great plays alike would be the talk of the esports community for a long time.

Most of the competitors in the first *Fortnite* World Cup finals were not especially famous at the time. But that would all change for the big winners. In the end, 16-year-old Kyle "Bugha" Giersdorf towered over the competition and won the Solo mode championship. No one else even came close to his top score. Overnight, he became a millionaire and one of the *Fortnite* community's biggest celebrities. It was a huge moment for *Fortnite* fans and esports in general.

The Secrets of Success

What makes a top esports player? It's more than just skills. To win big events, players need to be able to stay calm under pressure. No matter how good someone is or how much they practice, they won't be able to compete if they can't stay focused. Next time you watch an esports event, notice how the players keep their eyes locked on their screens. You've probably also noticed that they almost always wear headphones. This helps them concentrate by blocking noise and other distractions.

CHAPTER 4

Breaking Down Barriers

Sometimes the excitement around an esports match doesn't come from the action itself, but from the people playing. One great example took place at the 2019 Evo Japan event. Like the main Evo event held each year in the United States, Evo Japan is a huge tournament where players come from all over to compete in a number of fighting games. But due to the location, most competitors tend to come from Japan or nearby South Korea.

Evo events are open to anyone who wants to compete. They don't require players to be well known or established. This means that technically anyone could have a shot at winning. But most of the time, the top honors go to famous players. The very best players are more likely to have competed in other events and gained a reputation. But this wasn't the case in 2019.

The gaming industry is huge in Japan.

At the event, a player named Arslan "Arslan Ash" Siddique took everyone by surprise and dominated the *Tekken 7* tournament. For most fans, Siddique seemed to come out of nowhere. He hadn't competed in many events before. He also came from Pakistan, a country that is not well known for its fighting game scene.

Getting from Pakistan to Japan was difficult for Siddique. First, he had trouble getting a **visa** so he could enter Japan. Then his actual trip turned out to be tough. Siddique had to take five

Mountain Dew has become a big sponsor of esports tournaments and teams.

different flights to reach Japan, and he experienced delays along the way. The journey took him more than 2 full days. He finally arrived with only an hour to go before he had to start playing.

Though he was tired and stressed out from his difficult travel experience, Siddique showed no signs of struggle. He defeated many of the world's top *Tekken* players and secured the championship.

Siddique credited his win to his fellow players back home in Pakistan. He had trained against them for years, and many of them were also highly skilled. They simply hadn't had the chance to show off their abilities on the big stage in front of international audiences. But since Siddique's win, many in the fighting game scene are paying more attention to Pakistan. Several other Pakistani players have started to make names for themselves in pro tournaments. Siddique went on to win the *Tekken 7* championship at the U.S. Evo event a few months after the one in Japan.

Career Moves

After Siddique won at Evo Japan 2019, he was able to sign some big **sponsorship** deals. He became a huge star almost overnight. This meant he would never have to worry about being able to make it to the next major tournament. Back in his hometown of Lahore, Pakistan, he is a local celebrity. "When I go to a shopping mall, everyone comes up to me," he said in an interview.

In 2019, the all-female group Team Dignitas won their second straight Intel Challenge World Championship in Katowice, Poland.

In general, most esports competitors are male. But lately, that's been changing. In 2018, Kim "Geguri" Se-yeon became the first woman to play in the *Overwatch* League, a pro league devoted to the team-based shooting game *Overwatch*. The same year, Sasha "Scarlett" Hostyn became the first woman to win a major *StarCraft II* competition.

In 2019, Xiaomeng "VKLiooon" Li became the first woman to win the *Hearthstone* Grandmasters Global Finals, the major championship of the card-based video game *Hearthstone*. After winning, she offered inspiring words to young girls watching the match. "If you want to do it and believe in yourself," she said, "you should just forget your gender and go for it."

With so many new people getting into esports all the time, the future is sure to be very exciting. Competition will get even more intense. New records will be set, and new stars will be born. There's no way to predict what will happen next, but that's part of the fun. Keep watching!

Think About It

Try exploring esports history for yourself. Go online and look up videos of the events mentioned in this book. Or look up videos of players and games that you already follow. As you watch, try to answer these questions:

- Which moments are most exciting to you? Do these moments have anything in common?

- Do you think some types of games are more exciting to watch than others? Why?

- Would you share any of these videos with someone who doesn't already watch esports? How would you explain the videos so they make sense to an esports beginner?

For More Information

BOOKS

Austic, Greg. *Game Design.* Ann Arbor, MI: Cherry Lake Publishing, 2013.

Reeves, Diane Lindsey. *Find Your Future in Technology.* Ann Arbor, MI: Cherry Lake Publishing, 2016.

Trueit, Trudi Strain. *Video Gaming.* Ann Arbor, MI: Cherry Lake Publishing, 2008.

WEBSITES

Mixer
www.mixer.com
This interactive livestreaming service by Microsoft is home to a few of the biggest names in game streaming.

Twitch
www.twitch.tv
Check out some streams for yourself on the most popular streaming service.

GLOSSARY

combo (KAHM-boh) a series of attacks strung together in a fighting game

commentators (KAH-muhn-tay-turz) people who talk about a live sporting event as it happens, to make the event more interesting and exciting for viewers

esports (EE-sports) the sport of professional video game competitions

parry (PAIR-ee) to deflect an attack

rivalries (RYE-vuhl-reez) strong, lasting competitive relationships between certain players or teams

sponsorship (SPAHN-sur-ship) an arrangement where a player or team receives money from a company in exchange for advertising the company's products while playing

visa (VEE-zuh) a document allowing someone from one country to visit another and stay for a certain amount of time

INDEX